YUKO SHIRAISHI

Assemble - Disperse

3 May - 2 June 2001

Annely Juda Fine Art
23 Dering Street (off New Bond Street)
London W1S 1AW
Tel   020 7629 7578   Fax   020 7491 2139
Monday - Friday 10 - 6   Saturday 10 - 1

cover: Installation at Annely Juda Fine Art 2001

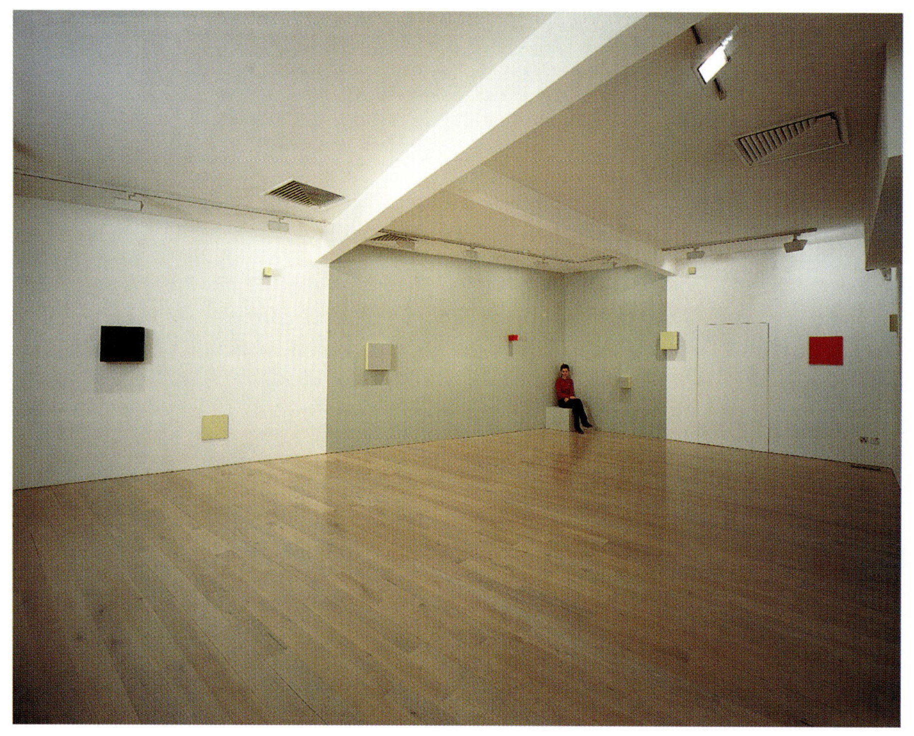

Installation at Annely Juda Fine Art 2001

I left Japan in 1974. I lived in Vancouver for three years and then, in 1977, came to London. I've now spent more than half my life in the West. I used to be asked about the influence of western culture on my work and how my work reflects my Japanese background and identity. Perhaps because of the ever increasing globalisation of the world, I'm not asked these questions so much these days.

Globalisation, Identity, Culture, Art and A World of My Own

One way in which I relate to the world at large is to use the internet to find out what is going on by way of art, culture and all sorts of other things. But I know I am just licking the cream on the cake. It has a quick, sweet, artificial taste - nothing more, nothing less.

I was eighteen when I left Japan and came face to face with a culture very different from my own. This made me aware of my own roots. Eiji Yoshikawa, a popular Japanese writer of historical fiction, once remarked that travelling abroad was like standing between a pair of mirrors - you don't just see yourself from in front, but also from behind. A foreign culture is like a mirror that helps you reflect on yourself in all sorts of new and different ways. It also makes you aware of the commonality that exists between different peoples and cultures.

I recently saw Ang Lee's *Crouching Tiger, Hidden Dragon*. This highly enjoyable film successfully combines, as the director intended, popular entertainment with art-house aesthetics. What really interests me is Ang Lee's expression of biculturalism and bilingualism. It represents, I think, a new cultural form. Born in Taiwan, he has lived in the USA since 1978. He has made western films like *The Ice Storm* and *Sense and Sensibility* as well as Asian films such as *Eat, Drink, Man, Woman*. He explores from a trans-cultural position his concern with the human condition and the tensions, for example, between morality and earthly desire.

Film-making is a multi-disciplinary art form involving the visual, the literary, the musical and the temporal. An episode that comes to mind happened during my first visit to England, when I was nineteen years old. I had the chance to meet Stanley Kubrick. Although an American, he lived much of his life in England. I remember very clearly how our conversation started. He was keen to know who was the most popular western film-maker in Japan - not so much among intellectuals as among the general public. I forget what I said, but we then started talking about *Dr. Strangelove*, which I said I very much admired. He asked whether I had watched the film in English or with Japanese sub-titles. I said with Japanese sub-titles, of course, because my English was so poor. He then spent at least half an hour explaining how much importance he attached to his scripts. He said that for him the spoken word was a key issue and that the essential starting point for his art was a good book or script. At the time he had just finished editing *Barry Lyndon*. Kubrick was extremely intelligent and sensitive in the way he used language to develop his plots and to explore the depths and twists of his characters' psychology. I've watched *Dr. Strangelove* over and over again. Each time, as my English ability has improved, I've been able to appreciate more directly the sophistication of the language Kubrick used.

I myself work in a medium that is untroubled by issues of translation. This isn't the case for writers, poets and film-makers. If they want to export their work to the wider world, they have to rely on the translated word. Visual artists and musicians, even if they do use language, are at less of a disadvantage. All the same, as my conversation with Kubrick so forcefully made me realise, culture is fundamentally rooted in language. When I switch between English and Japanese, I feel like two quite different people. Why is this, I wonder.

My work, as I've said, revolves around the use of visual language. I have a sense, though, that deep down my visual world is shaped by my experience of the spoken and written word. That is why language fascinates me so much. Language is culture. Western culture is built on languages that are strictly logical in nature. The way in which laws and contracts are used to sustain society comes from the belief that all phenomena can be explained in words. The supremacy accorded to language has also been responsible for the development of western analytic science.

In the East, on the other hand, comprehension is often sought through means other than language. There is the notion of *anmoku no ryokai* or tacit understanding, in which people communicate in silence - like insects reading each others' minds with their long antennae. There is also the idea that words themselves are charged with power. The Japanese term *kotodama* means spirit of the word or spirit of language. *Koto* is written with the first character of *kotoba*, which means word or language. The character *koto* can also be read *iu*, which means to speak. The character for dama is the same as that for tamashii, which means soul or spirit. *Kotodama* refers to the strange power which words are thought to possess.

Belief in the magical power of words is, of course, universal. In the ancient world knowing someone's name gave you a certain control over that person. For that reason people were reluctant to reveal their names to strangers. In Judaism, Jews were forbidden to pronounce God's name because any attempt to express it was bound to be inadequate. Written YHWH, God's name was never pronounced in any reading of the scriptures.

The idea that words are magical is something I learnt as a child. When I was five or six years old my mother told me that if I ever had a nightmare I should tell her what I had seen. She said that if I did this, what I had seen in my dream wouldn't come true. On the other hand, she said, if I had a good dream I shouldn't tell anyone about it. That way there would be a chance that the dream would come true. I still observe this maxim today. It has happened to me more than once that when I have spoken about something important, the magic has been lost and I have ended up feeling empty and deflated. This is why in principle I don't like to talk about my paintings.

In the story of Orpheus, he is told by the God of the Underworld that to bring his wife back from the dead he may lead her back to the world of the living on condition that he does not turn around and look at her before leaving the gates of hell. Orpheus is unable to restrain himself and at the last moment turns around, consigning his wife back to the realm of the dead and losing her forever. There is something of the Orpheus myth in me. There are times, of course, when the uttering of words generates enormous magical power. But in my case I prefer to follow the path of expression through silence. The existence in East Asia of terms such as *anmoku no ryokai*, tacit understanding, has much to do with the use of *kanji* or Chinese characters and the way in which they represent ideas through both sound and image.

Ten years ago my aunt suffered a stroke that damaged the left pre-central gyrus of her brain. The right hand side of her body was paralysed and she lost the power of speech. Although she understands what a desk is, for example, she can't say the word for it. On the other hand she can remember the Chinese character for desk because, being an ideogram, it resides in her visual memory. With *hiragana* and *katakana*, which are syllabaries, it doesn't work. So we communicate with each other by writing Chinese characters.

Michel Foucault, the French philosopher, has written:

But the history of a language endowed with a figurative writing soon comes to a halt. For it is hardly possible to achieve much progress in such a language. With alphabetic writing, in fact, the history of men is entirely changed. They transcribe in space, not their ideas but sounds, and from these sounds they extract the common elements in order to form a small number of unique signs whose combination will enable them to form all possible syllables and words. Alphabetical writing, by abandoning the attempt to draw the representation, transposes into its analysis of sounds the rules that are valid for reason itself. So that it does not matter that letters do not represent ideas, and ideas can be linked together and disjoined just like the letters of the alphabet. (The Order of Things)

And in the words of the Japanese scientist Takeshi Yoro:

If we Orientals have a predilection towards palmistry or the study of physiognomy, this is surely because we have been brought up using Chinese characters. We are very sensitive when it comes to finding meaning through visual observation. Cultures which use alphabets, on the other hand, tend to construct meaning through assemblages of parts. (Veins of the Brain)

These differences in the nature of eastern and western languages have given rise to different systems of philosophy. Both of these, not so much in the sense of my being bilingual, reside within me.

The hybrid culture of people like Ang Lee, whose film-making I referred to earlier, is rapidly becoming the defining feature of our age. Information swirls around us from every direction and we find ourselves located not so much between a pair of mirrors but at the centre of an infinitely faceted reflective globe. I am reminded of the character in a mystery story who goes mad after entering a sphere of mirrors. Ours is indeed an age of insanity and information overload in which we can observe ourselves from any number of directions. At the same time, however, we are afforded the ability to take a global overview of things. As Umberto Eco has stated:

Our century has perhaps been hypocritical, but it has been moral in equal measure. It is in this century that a sense of global solidarity has developed for the first time. (Conversations About the End of Time)

How do we come to a global understanding of our world? How, having licked off the cream, can we get to eat the cake itself? Human history may seem long, but in reality it is very short - the history of language and technology has hardly begun. With patience, dignity and flexibility we have to seek out from the chaos around us that which is quintessential. To identify and cultivate this is the great task that faces us. Human existence is the outcome of an extraordinary balance of microscopic forces involving cells, bodily fluids and micro-organisms. Our relationship with culture is no less intimate. Like food, we absorb it, are nourished by it and discard it as if it were an essential part of our metabolic functioning.

My hope is that the prejudices with which we find ourselves surrounded - religious bigotry, racial and sexual prejudice, and discrimination premised on genetic determinism - will gradually dissipate as we negotiate the chaotic multiculturalism and information overload of our times.

Yuko Shiraishi February 2001

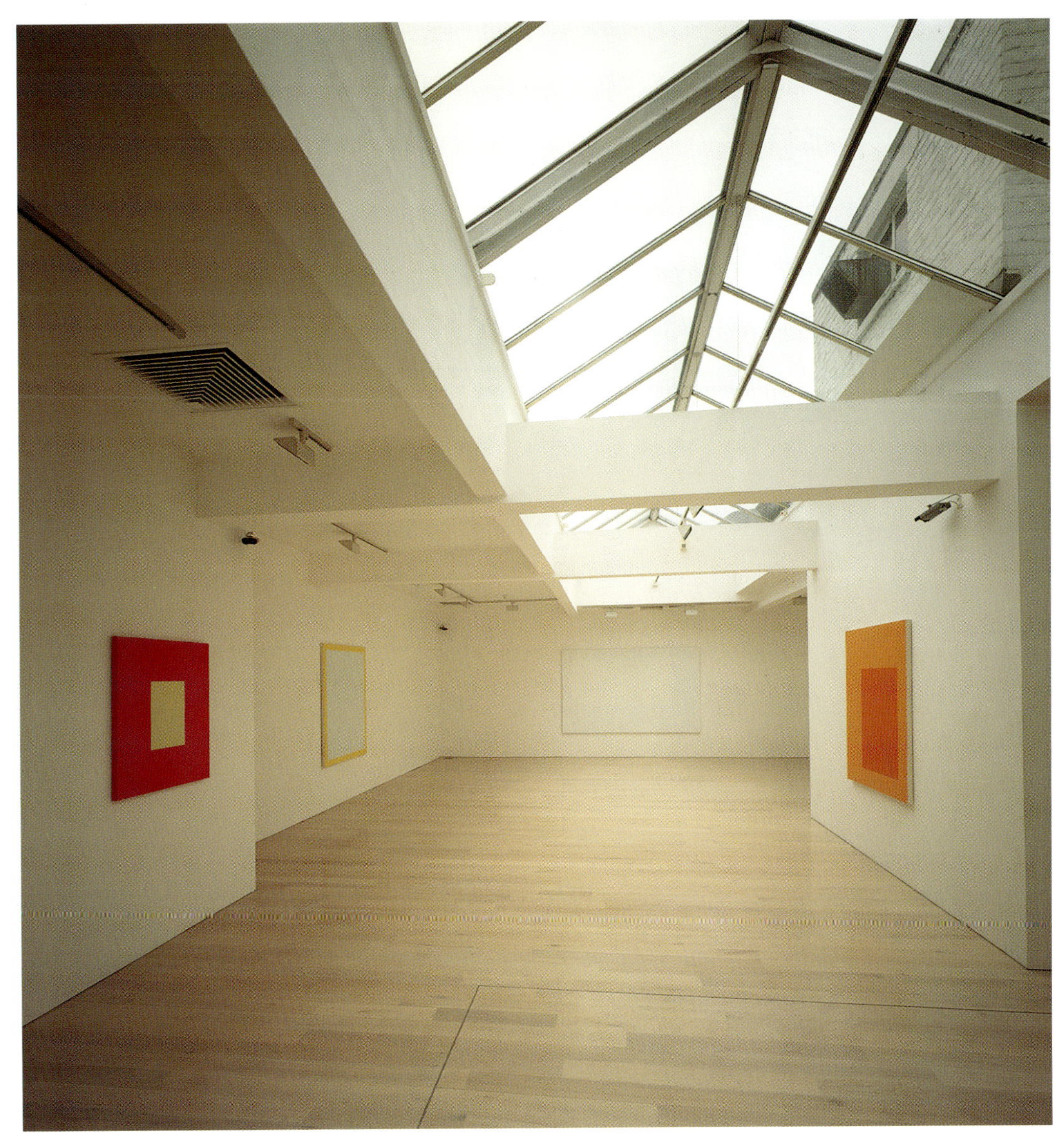

Installation at Annely
Juda Fine Art 2001

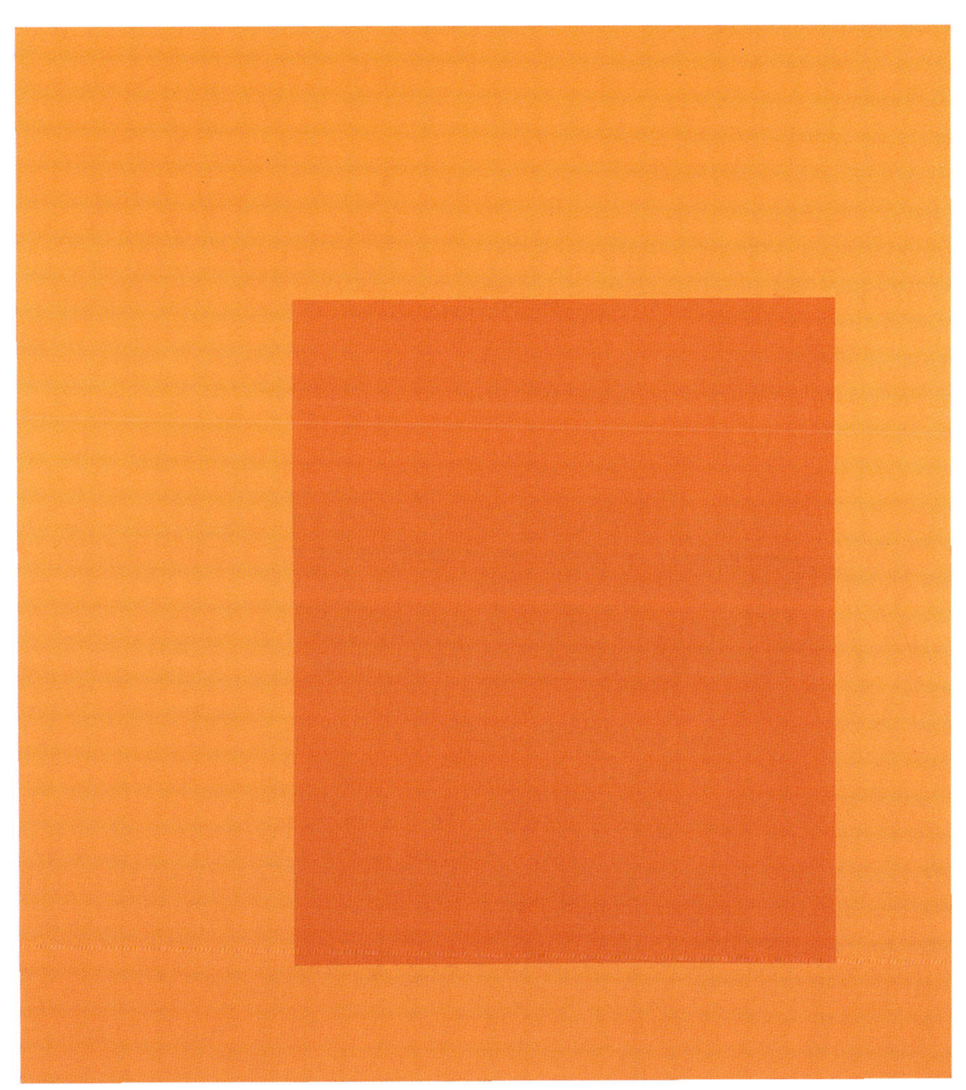

Halting Orange (2) 2000
oil on canvas
137 x 122 cm

Emerging White Square (2) 2000
oil on canvas
168 x 273 cm

Obtaining Black 2000
oil on canvas
89 x 81 cm

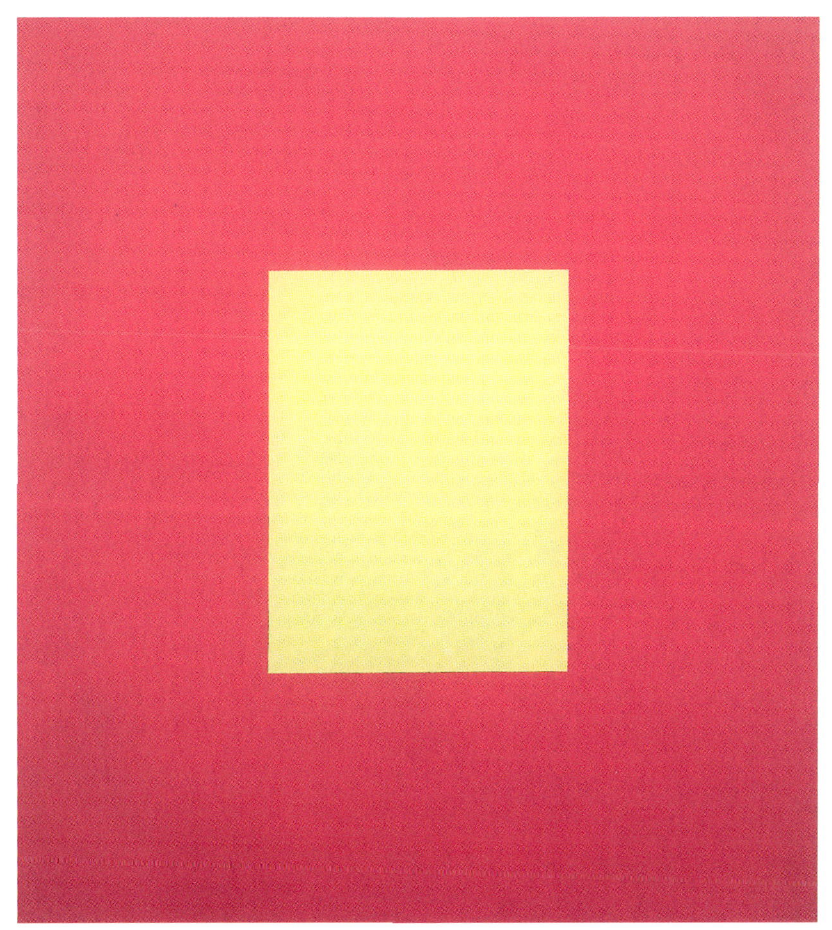

Halting Yellow 2000
oil on canvas
91 x 81 cm

Green Swallow 2000
oil on canvas
168 x 152 cm

Forest 2000
oil on canvas
152 x 137 cm

Flux 2000
oil on canvas
168 x 152 cm

Emerging White Square 2000
oil on canvas
168 x 273 cm

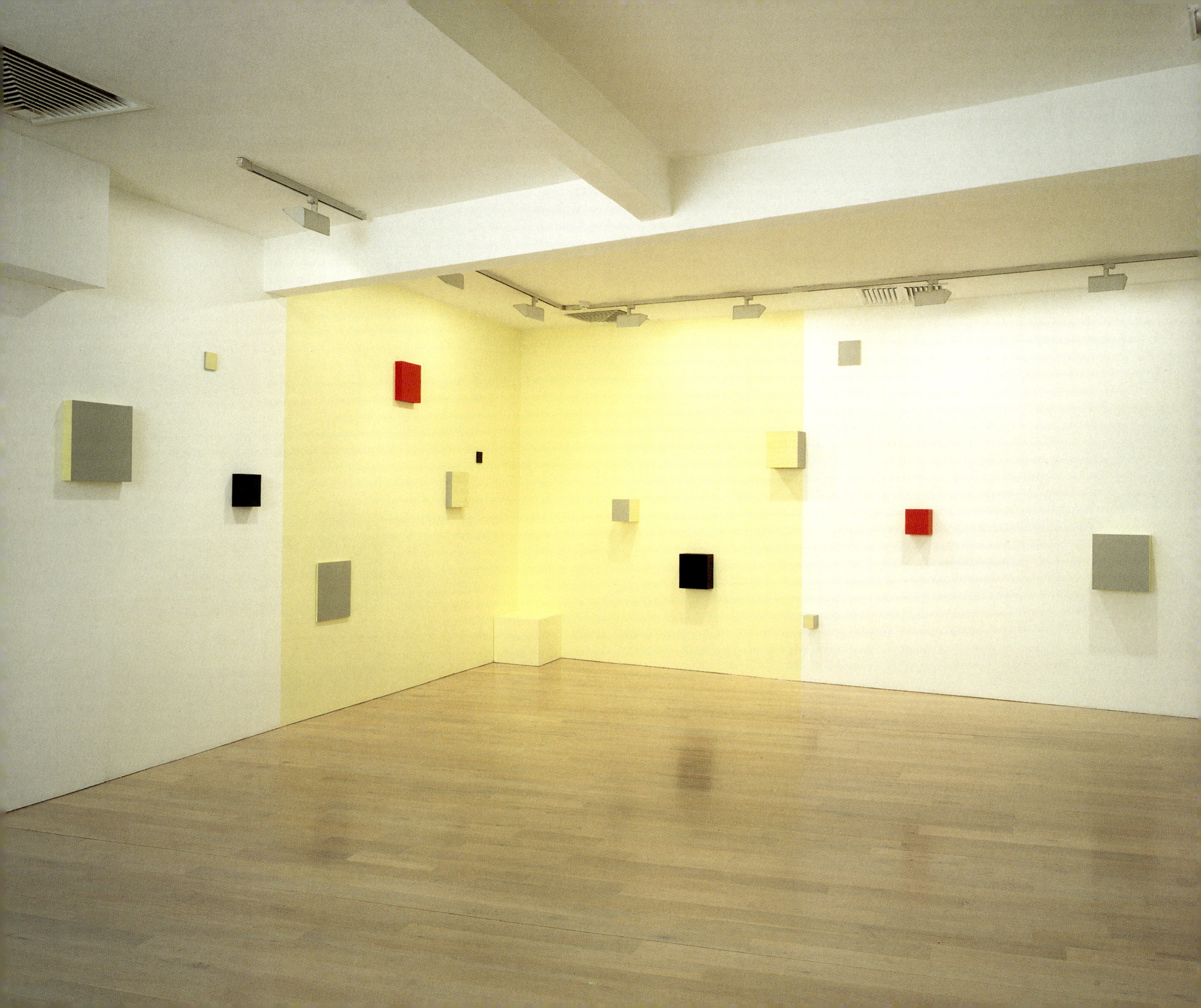

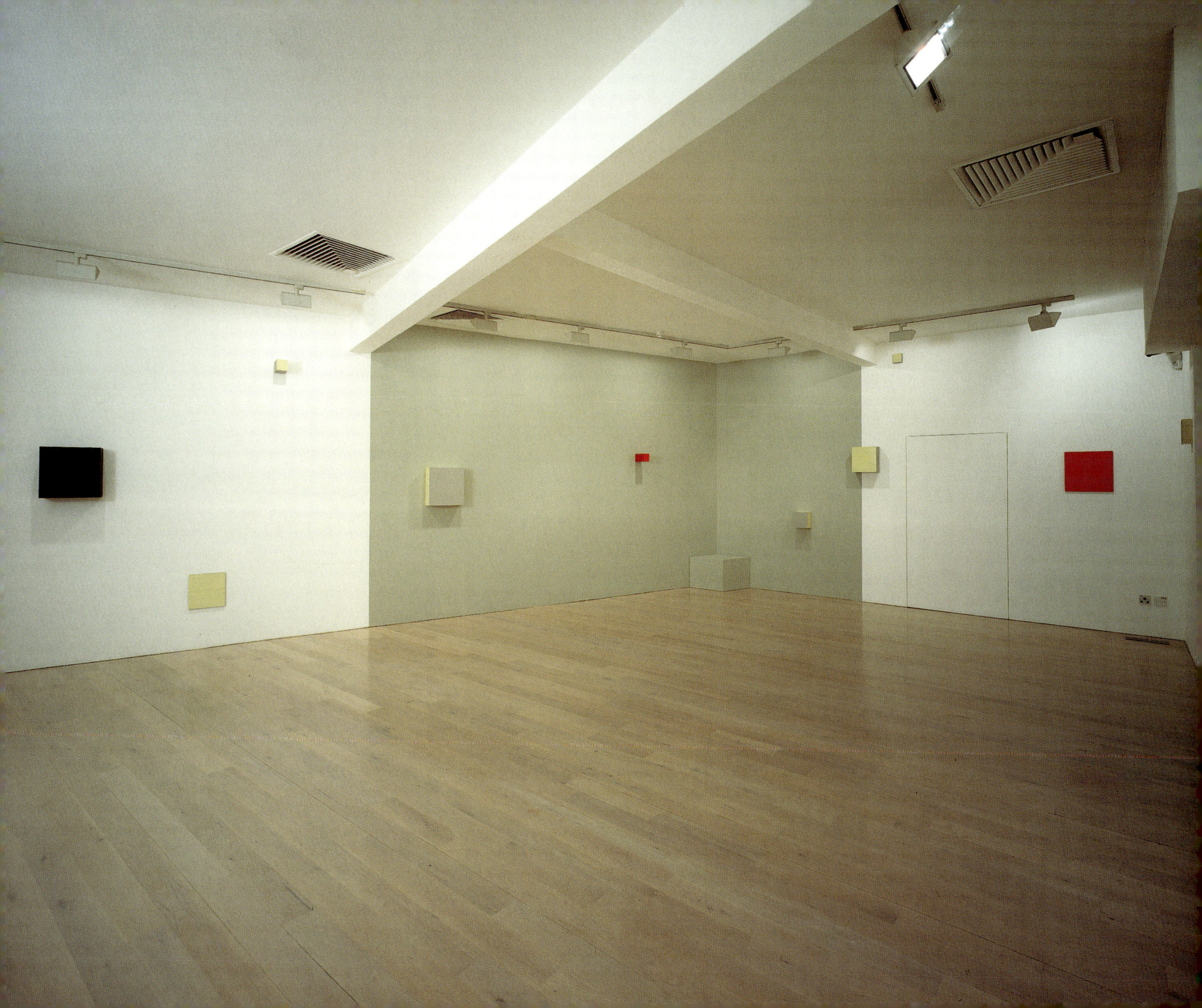

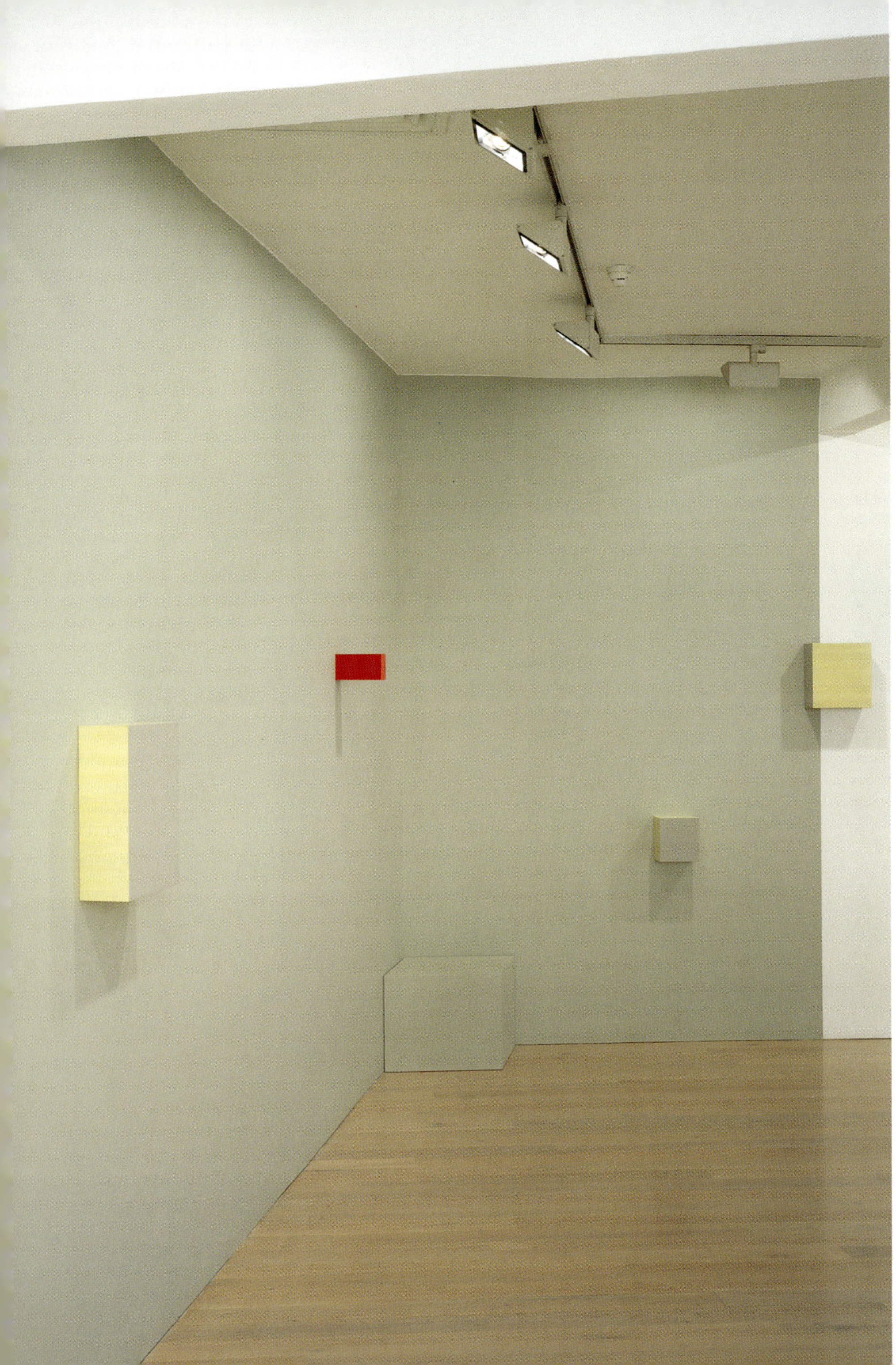

left, opposite and overleaf: Installation at Annely Juda Fine Art 2001, includes:

Assemble - Disperse (Pale Yellow and Pale Grey) I 2000, oil on wood, 8 parts
Assemble - Disperse (Pale Yellow and Pale Grey) II 2000, oil on wood, 8 parts
Red Squares 2000, oil on wood, 4 parts
Night Blue Squares 2000, oil on wood, 4 parts

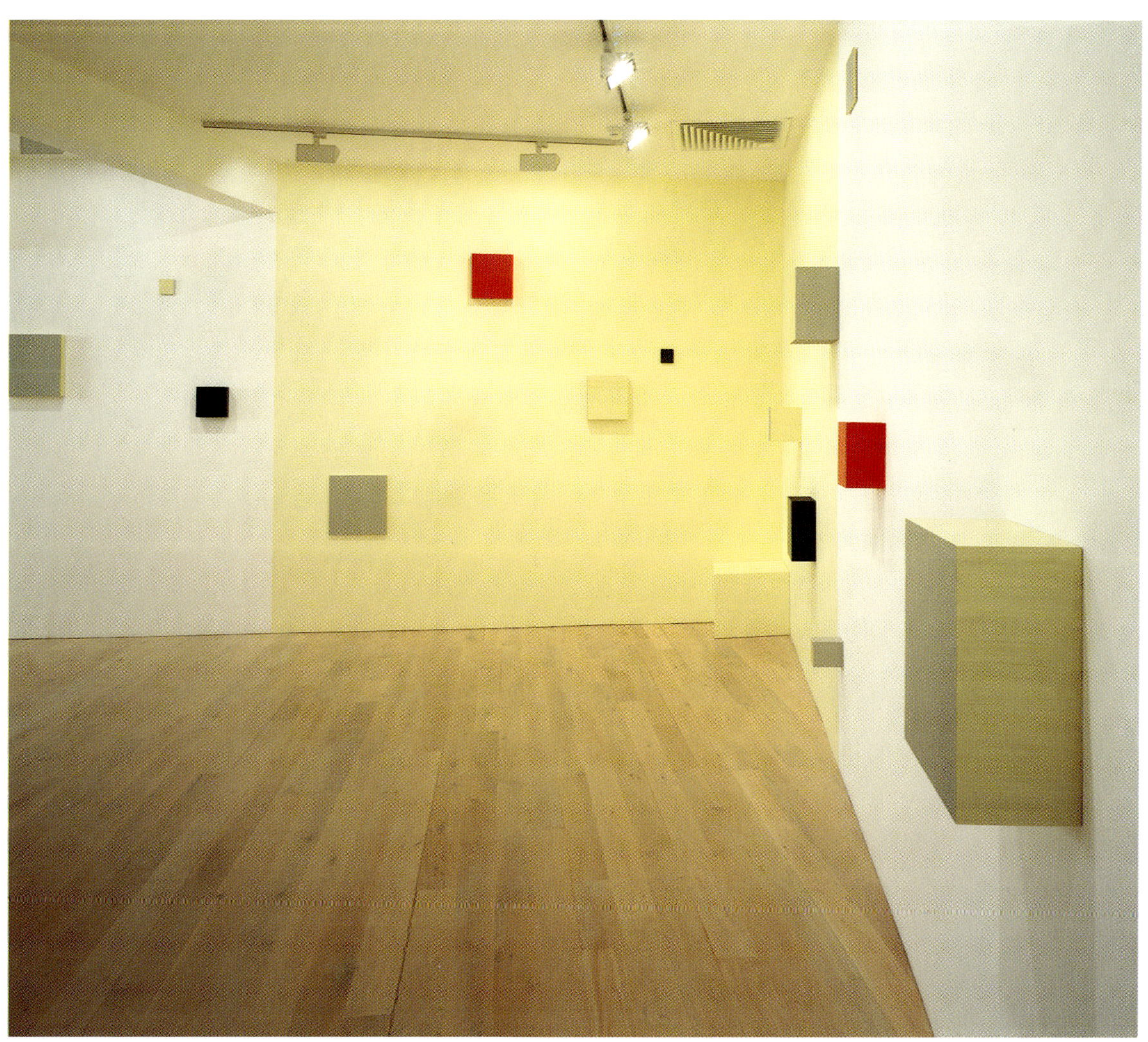

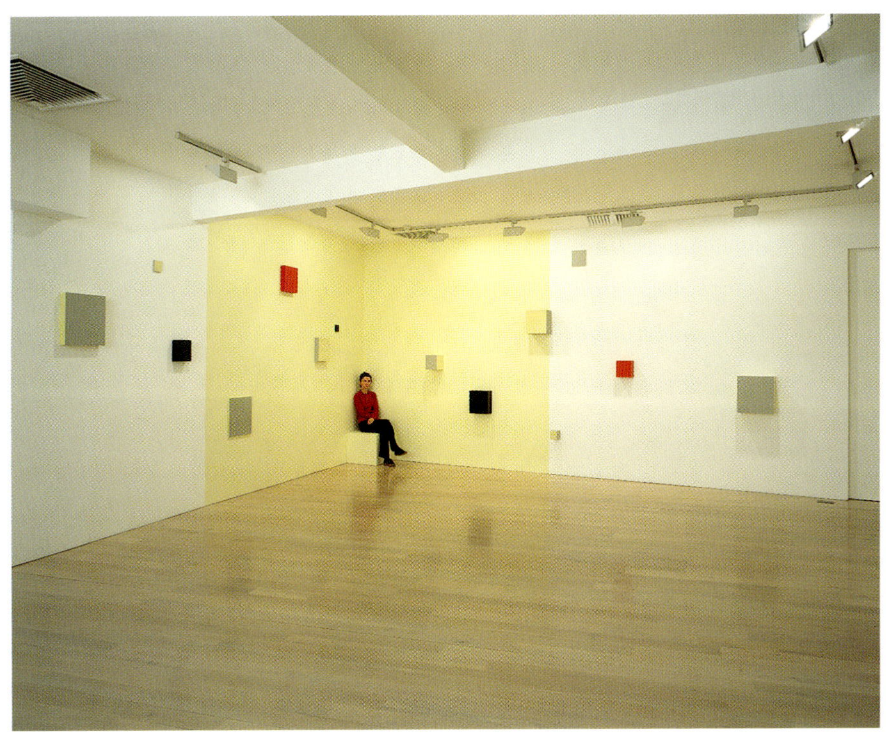

Installation at Annely Juda Fine Art 2001

<u>**Biography**</u>

1956   Born Tokyo
1974-76 Lived in Vancouver, Canada
1978-81 Chelsea School of Art, BA
1981-82 Chelsea School of Art, MA

Lives and works in London

<u>**One-person exhibitions**</u>

1984 Curwen Gallery, London
1988 Edward Totah Gallery, London
1989 Tieerhuys Galerij, Brugge, Belgium
      Shigeru Yokota Gallery, Tokyo, Japan
1990 Galerie Konstruktiv Tendens, Stockholm
      Edward Totah Gallery, London
      Artsite, Bath
1991 Margaret Lipworth Fine Art, Florida, USA
      Cairn Gallery, Nailsworth
1992 Galerie Lüpke, Frankfurt, Germany
      Shigeru Yokota Gallery, Tokyo, Japan
      Edward Totah Gallery, London
1993 Gallery Kasahara, Osaka, Japan
      Slade Gallery, University College, London
1994 Galerie Konstruktiv Tendens, Stockholm
      ACP Viviane Ehrli Galerie, Zurich, Switzerland
1996 ACP Viviane Ehrli Galerie, Zurich, Switzerland
      Galerie Hans Mayer, Düsseldorf, Germany
      Gallery Kasahara, Osaka, Japan
      Experimental Art Foundation, Adelaide,
      Australia
1997 Galerie Konstruktiv Tendens, Stockholm
      Shigeru Yokota Gallery, Tokyo, Japan
      Annely Juda Fine Art, London
1998 ACP Viviane Ehrli Galerie, Zurich, Switzerland
      Ernst Museum, Budapest, Hungary

1999 Nancy Hoffman Gallery, New York
      As Dark as Light, Tate Gallery St Ives, St Ives
      International, Cornwall
2000 Galerie Konstruktiv Tendens, Stockholm
2001 Assemble-Disperse, Annely Juda Fine Art,
      London

<u>**Projects**</u>

2001 FIH: Field Institute Hombroich (with
      Tadashi Kawamata, Katsuhito Nishikawa)
      Stiftung Insel Hombroich Museum,
      Neuss, Germany

<u>**Selected Group Exhibitions**</u>

1980 New Contemporaries, ICA, London
1981 Contemporary Japanese Prints Royal Academy
      of Arts, London
1983 Nantenshi Gallery, Tokyo, Japan Galerie 39,
      London
      International European Print Exhibition,
      Musée d'Art Moderne, Liège, Belgium
1985 Japanesque, Mostyn Art Gallery, Llandudno,
      Wales
      Whitechapel Open Exhibition, London
      The Camden Annual, Camden Arts Centre,
      London
      International Biennale of Graphic Art,
      Moderna Galeria, Ljubljana, former
      Jugoslavia (representing Great Britain)
      Day 1st Art, Liget Galeria, Budapest, Hungary
1986 The Camden Annual, Camden Arts Centre,
      London
      Arts of Today, Budapest Gallery, Hungary

1988 Nancy Hoffman Gallery, New York
     The Presence of Painting: Aspects of British
     Abstraction 1957-88; Arts Council Touring
     Exhibition, Mappin Art Gallery, Sheffield
     Hatton Art Gallery, Newcastle Ikon Gallery,
     Birmingham
1989 Whitechapel Open, Whitechapel Art Gallery,
     London
     From Prism to Paintbox, Colour Theory and
     Practice in Modern British Painting, Oriel
     Gallery, Clwyd, Wales
     Galerie Konstruktiv Tendens, Stockholm
1990 Künstlerinnen des 20 Jahrhunderts,
     Museum Wiesbaden, Germany
     Galerie Konstruktiv Tendens, Stockholm
     Whitechapel Open, Whitechapel Art Gallery,
     London
1991 Galerie Konstruktiv Tendens, Stockholm
     Double Take, American-Japan Art Association,
     New York
1992 Geteilte Bilder - Das Diptychon in der neuen
     Kunst, Folkwang Museum, Essen, Germany
     A Sense of Purpose, Mappin Art Gallery,
     Sheffield
     Whitechapel Open, Whitechapel Art Gallery,
     London
     The Solstice, Cairn Gallery, Nailsworth
     The 20th Anniversary Exhibition,
     Gallery Kasahara, Osaka, Japan
     Galerie Konstruktiv Tendens, Stockholm
1993 Moving into View - Recent British Painting,
     Arts Council Touring Exhibition
     The Structure of Painting - Japanese
     Contemporary Stripes, Bumpodo Gallery,
     Tokyo, Japan

Zwei Energien, Haus für Konstruktive und
Konkrete Kunst, Zurich, Switzerland
Contemporary Art, Courtauld Institute, London
Geometric Abstraktion XII, Galerie
Konstruktiv Tendens, Stockholm
1994 Lead and Follow, Bade Gallery, Jarrow
     Atlantis Gallery, London
     Painters and Prints, Curwen Gallery, London
     Unveiled, Cornerhouse Gallery, Manchester
     New Painting (Arts Council Collection)
     Darlington Arts Centre, Darlington
     Oriel Gallery, Clwyd, Wales
     Jerwood Painting Prize 1994 - Royal Scottish
     Academy, Edinburgh; Royal Academy of Arts,
     London
     Surface Tensions, Curwen Gallery, London
     Geometric Abstraktion XIII, Galerie
     Galerie Konstruktiv Tendens, Stockholm
1995 Walk-in Sculpture, Shigeru Yokota Gallery,
     Tokyo, Japan
     New Painting (Arts Council of Great Britain):
     University Gallery, Newcastle Upon Tyne;
     Norwich Gallery; The Drumcroon Gallery,
     Wigan
     Pretext Heteronyms, Clink Street Studios,
     London, curated by Rear Window
     White Out, Curwen Gallery, London
     Geometric Abstraktion XIV, Galerie
     Konstruktiv Tendens, Stockholm
1996 New Painting from the Arts Council
     Collection, Bath Museum
     The 10th Anniversary Exhibition, ACP
     Vivian Ehrli Galerie, Zurich, Switzerland
     Geometric Abstraktion XV, Galerie Konstruktiv
     Tendens, Stockholm

1997 Pretext Heteronyms, San Michele, Rome, Italy
Off the Wall, Nancy Hoffman Gallery, New York
New Acquisitions, Daimler Benz, Stuttgart, Germany
Geometric Abstraktion XVI, Galerie Konstruktiv Tendens, Stockholm
Haus Bill, Zumikon, Zurich, Switzerland

1998 Clear and Saturated, Arti et Amicitiae, Amsterdam, Netherlands
The 25th Anniversary Exhibition, Nancy Hoffman Gallery, New York
Immerzeit, Forum Konkrete Kunst Galerie am Fischmarkt, Erfurt, Germany
Geometric Abstraktion XVII, Galerie Konstruktiv Tendens, Stockholm

1999 Geometrie als Gestalt, Neue Nationalgalerie, Berlin, Germany
A Line in Painting, Gallery Fine, London
Vendégjáték, Ernst Museum, Budapest, Hungary
The Equinox, Cairn Gallery, Nailsworth
Gateways, Nancy Hoffman Gallery, New York
Geometric Abstraktion XVIII, Galerie Konstruktiv Tendens, Stockholm
Engaging Tradition, Hotbath Gallery, Bath
White Out, Gallery Fine, London

2000 Blue: Borrowed and New, The New Art Gallery, Walsall
The Framed Image, Nancy Hoffman Gallery, New York
Grau ist nicht Grau, Galerie Gisele Linder, Basel, Switzerland
Underlying Perfection, Gallery Fine, London
Geometric Abstraktion XIX, Galerie Konstruktiv Tendens, Stockholm

Public Collections

Arthur Anderson Collection, London and Stockholm
Arts Council of Great Britain
British Council, London
British Government Collection, London
British Museum, London
Contemporary Art Society, London
Daimler Benz, Stuttgart
Graphische Sammlung Albertina, Vienna
Graves City Art Gallery, Sheffield
IBM, London
London & Continental Bankers, Ltd
Ludwig Museum, Budapest
Max Bill - George Vantongerloo Foundation, Zumikon, Switzerland
McCrory Corporation, New York
Ohara Museum, Japan
Ove Arup, London
Seibu, Japan
Unilever, London
Weishaupt Forum, Ulm, Germany
YKK, Japan

Selected Bibliography

1988 'The Presence of Painting' catalogue essay by Michael Tooby, 'Aspects of British Abstraction 1957-1988', Mappin Art Gallery, Sheffield

1989 Tieerhuys Galerij, Belgium, catalogue essay by Yuko Shiraishi
'Yuko Shiraishi' catalogue essay by Michael Tooby, Shigeru Yokota Gallery, Tokyo

'From Prism to Paintbox - Colour Theory
and Practice in Modern British Painting'
catalogue essay by Roy Osborne, Oriel
Gallery, Clwyd, Wales

1990 'Yuko Shiraishi' catalogue essay by Margaret
Garlake, Edward Totah Gallery, London
'Künstlerinnen des 20 Jahrhunderts'
catalogue essay by Sister Wendy Beckett,
Museum Wiesbaden, Germany

1991 'Double Take Japan - America' catalogue essay
by Michael Tooby and Akira Tatehata, Art
Association, New York

1992 'Gesteilte Bilder-Das Diptychon in der
neuen Kunst' catalogue essay by Gerhard
Finckh, Museum Folkwang, Essen, Germany
'A sense of purpose' catalogue essay by
Michael Tooby, Mappin Art Gallery, Sheffield
Sister Wendy Beckett, 'Art and the Sacred',
published by Dorling Kindersley

1993 'Yuko Shiraishi' catalogue essay by Mel
Gooding, Gallery Kasahara, Osaka, Japan
'Moving into View - Recent British
painting' catalogue essay by Sacha Craddock,
Arts Council, London
'The Structure of Painting - Japanese
Contemporary Stripes' catalogue essay by
Arta Tani, Bumpodo Gallery, Tokyo
'Zwei Energien', Haus für Konstruktive und
Konkrete Kunst, Zurich: catalogue essay by
Thomas A. Clark; 'Japan Aspekte Eines Landes
und Einer Gesellschaft' by Margit Staber-
Weinberg
'Junge Kunst Sammeln 93' catalogue essay
by Heinrich Klotz, Daimler Benz, Stuttgart

1995 Sister Wendy Beckett, 'Meditations of Silence',
published by Dorling Kindersley

1996 Monograph 'Yuko Shiraishi', Cantz'sche
Verlag, Germany: 'Harmony That Puts Order
into Contradiction' by Dr Volker Rattemayer;
'Natural Selection' by Waldemar Januszczak;
'A Thin Irregular Yellow Line' by Thomas A.
Clark; 'Torrential Rain' by Yuko Shiraishi
'Focus' catalogue essay by Richard Grayson:
'"Not quite" Some works by Yuko Shiraishi',
'Focus' catalogue essay by Yuko Shiraishi,
Experimental Art Foundation, Australia

1997 'Heteronymous' catalogue essay by Achille
Bonito Oliva
Juliet Steyu and Stella Santacatterina
'Juxtapositions' catalogue essay by Caoímhin
Mac Giolla Léith, Annely Juda Fine Art,
London

1998 'Abstraction and Melancholy' catalogue
essay by Ildikó D. Udvary
'Yuko Shiraishi' catalogue essay by Norbert
Lynton, Ernst Museum, Budapest
'Clear and Saturated' catalogue essay by Yuko
Shiraishi Arti et Amicitiae, Amsterdam
'Innerscape - Anthology of Artists' Writings'
edited by Maurizio Pellegrin, Trieste, Italy

1999 'As Dark as Light', catalogue interview with
Michael Tooby, Tate St Ives, Cornwall
'Geometrie als Gestalt' catalogue essay by
Fritz Jacobi, Nationalgalerie, Berlin

2001 Assemble - Disperse catalogue essay by Yuko
Shiraishi: 'Globalisation, Identity, Culture, Art
and A World of My Own', Annely Juda Fine
Art, London

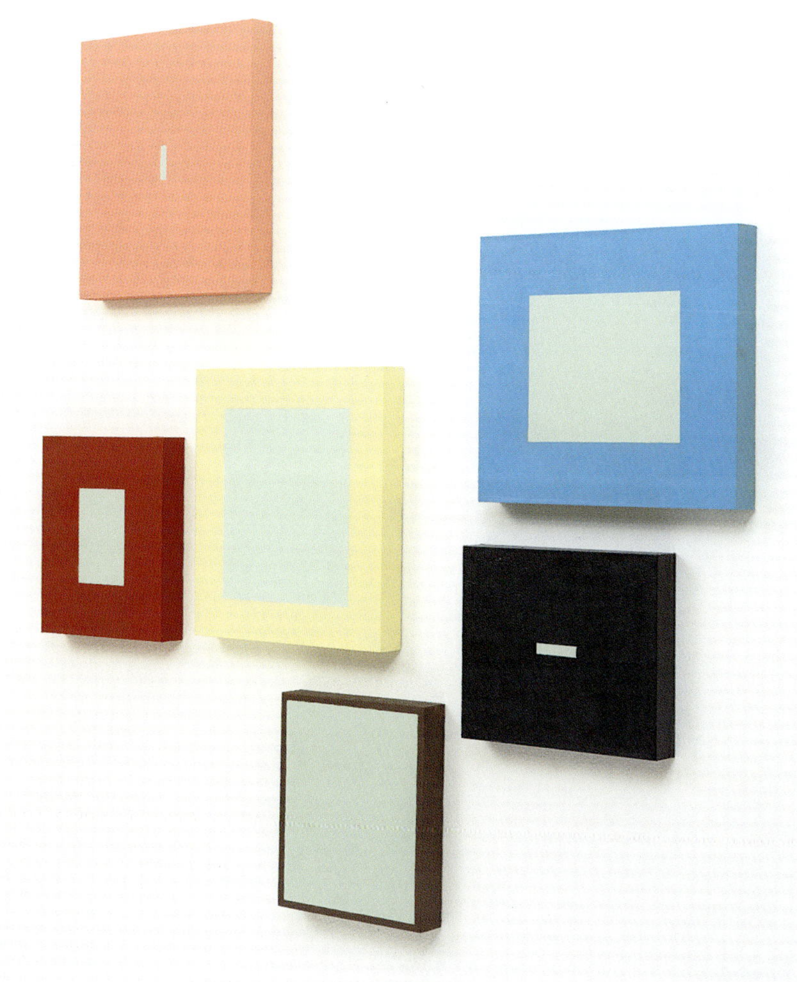

Disperse Squares 2000
oil on canvas, 6 parts
overall 120 x 120 cm

ISBN   1 870280 849

Photographs: Beatrice Behlen
               John Riddy
               Peter White
Catalogue © Annely Juda Fine Art/Yuko Shiraishi 2001

Printed by BAS Printers Ltd, England